Ka

Maya Chowdhry is an award-winning poet and playwright. She writes lyrical drama for radio, the Web, the page and stage. Her writing career began when she won the BBC Radio Young Playwrights Festival in 1991 with *Monsoon* and the Cardiff International Poetry Competition in 1992 with *Brides of Dust*. Her first stage play *Kaahini* was nominated for Best Children's Theatre by The Writers' Guild.

She has continually crossed boundaries and produced vibrant challenging work. In 2000 she received a *Year of the Artist* Research & Development Award for *Destiny*, a digital poetic tapestry. As an inTer-aCt-ive artist her recent online writing includes www.foundland.net, an Internet writing collaboration, and she was KODE Electronic Writer-in-Residence with Jubilee Arts www.kodewords.net.

Her stage plays include: *The Crossing Path* (The National Theatre: *Shell Connections*), *Playing With Fire* (TAG Theatre), *Sanctuary*, a multi-level interactive theatre experience (Yorkshire Women Theatre), *Seeing* (workshopped at The Royal Court Theatre), *Kaahini* (Birmingham Repertory Company, Red Ladder Theatre Company; National Tour), *An Appetite for Living* (West Yorkshire Playhouse), *Splinters* (Bradford Theatre in the Mill / Talawa Theatre at The Lyric Studio). She was writer-on-attachment at the National Theatre Studio in 2002.

Kaahini

by Maya Chowdhry

Capercaillie Books

CAPERCAILLIE BOOKS LIMITED

Published by Capercaillie Books Limited,

Registered Office 48 North Castle Street, Edinburgh.

© 2004 Capercaillie Books Limited.

The moral right of the author has been asserted.

Design by Ian Kirkwood Design.

Printed and bound in Great Britain by Antony Rowe Ltd., Chippenham, Wiltshire

Set in Cosmos and Veljovic

A catalogue record for this book is available from the British Library ISBN 0-9545206-4-5.

This book is sold subject to the condition that it shall not by way of trade or otherwise, be lent, resold, hired out or otherwise circulated without the publisher's prior consent in any form of binding or cover other than that in which it is published and without a similar condition including this condition being imposed on the subsequent purchaser.

All rights reserved. No part of this publication may be reproduced, stored in a retrieval system or transmitted in any form or by any means, electronic, mechanical or otherwise without the written permission of the publisher.

All applications for a licence to perform this play must be made to the Publishers at their Registered Office. No performance may take place unless a licence has been obtained.

The Publisher acknowledges support from the Scottish Arts Council towards the publication of this title.

For Anna and Yasmin Ashby

Introduction

. . . are we able to play with our gender and sexuality?

It seems in the intervening years between writing *Kaahini* and its publication that boundaries have been crossed and views stretched, but the story at the heart of *Kaahini* resonates across the years into an imagined future where possibilities defy cultural stereotypes, gender roles and sexualities.

I wrote *Kaahini* because I am interested in identities; in the fluidity of the myriad of aspects that make up our identities, the narrowness of gender roles and the osmotic relationship between culture and identity.

I have spent thirty-nine years searching for my identity and have discovered many identities which have changed over the years. I've uncovered inner and outer identities and unearthed an ability to transform according to the landscape of my life.

Unpicking my identity has been a matter of survival for me: sifting through the identities assigned to me by society; transforming and coming to an understanding of who I am; emerging defiantly opposite the image society has projected on me to be who I want to be.

In researching this play I have uncovered shamanic rituals in which men and women exchange genders. I have explored Hindu philosophy which recounts how the 'self' moves into time and emotions, feels desire and splits into male and female at the beginning of the world. Reflecting on the genderless nature of 'the soul' I reread the tale of Sikhandin in 'The Mahabharata', where King Drupada brings up his daughter as a son after a dream in which Shiva tells him his Queen is bearing a son. I thought about the implications of the legacy of the 'Ramayana'; boys are told to be like Rama and girls to be like Sita, and the taboos this puts in place.

In finding the story of *Kaahini* I wanted to put some of the ideas and information I've gained working with young Asian people into a play for and about their experiences, yet it was essential for me to push the boundaries of familiar themes and stories and find an exciting contemporary place to play.

The play contains only the essential directions for the action, which allows the director more freedom of interpretation in staging the play. When I write I see the play in an almost dream-like state yet I am always delightfully surprised by the look and feel of the production. Kully Thiarai, who directed *Kaahini* at Red Ladder Theatre Company worked with designer Kamini Gupta to produce an impressionistic set complete with musical soundtrack, while Indhu Rubasingham, director, and Nancy Surman, designer, produced a more naturalistic set complete with railway tracks running up centre stage for the production by the Birmingham Rep.

Kaahini was commissioned and developed by Red Ladder Theatre Company and toured nationally. It premiered at Bradford Theatre in the Mill in May 1997. The company wanted a play about identity that spoke specifically to young Asian women. The Birmingham Rep re-staged the play in 1998. The play was nominated for Best Children's Theatre by the Writers Guild.

Maya Chowdhry, 2004

Note on first production

Note: Kaahini was first produced by Red Ladder Theatre Company. It premiered at Bradford Theatre in the Mill, May 1997.

Esha: Nina Bhirangi

Farooq: Ashmeed Sohoye

Anishaa: Deni Francis

Neelendra: John Leery

Director: Kully Thiarai

Designer: Kamini Gupta

Dramaturgy: Noel Greig

Costumes: Mary Robson

Music: Akintayo Akinbode

Choreography: Greta Mendez

Lighting design: David Martin

Tour Manager: Stefanie Gascoigne

www.redladder.co.uk

Characters

ESHA:	an Asian teenager.
FAROOQ:	an Asian teenager, Esha's best friend.
ANISHAA:	Esha's mum, in her early thirties.
NEELENDRA:	Esha's dad, in his mid thirties.
MYSTIC:	Old man Neelendra and Anishaa visit. (can be played by Farooq's character)

Scene 1
(Prologue)

NEELENDRA, a young Asian man (17), wearing kurta pyjama, and ANISHAA, a young Asian woman (16), wearing a lavish salwaar kameez and a duputta, weave in and out of a fair, the sounds fill the night air.

They enter a tent and sit cross-legged. The MYSTIC is obscured, a small fire separates them, it emits a clear orange flame with little smoke which glows in the dark.

MYSTIC: Tell me your troubles.

NEELENDRA: I don't have any.

MYSTIC: Then why have you come?

ANISHAA: He's had this dream and wants to know — (what it means).

NEELENDRA: Nisha!

MYSTIC: Speak.

NEELENDRA: Well I dreamt, it felt like I was a (**pause**) woman in the dream and I was about to give birth. I look down to see that my belly has split open, blood surges out like a huge wave, it seems like my whole self is draining away. Then er . . .

NEELENDRA is sweating and mops his brow with a handkerchief, he looks at ANISHAA.

ANISHAA: There was a, er, serpent.

NEELENDRA: Suddenly there is this sea serpent drinking the blood from my open belly. Then I watch a buffalo leave from the same wound, it floats up into the air and I know it's my soul.

ANISHAA glances at NEELENDRA slightly surprised by the vivid description.

MYSTIC: How did you feel about this dream?

NEELENDRA: I didnt really think about it.

The MYSTIC chants quietly. A column of incense spirals into the air. NEELENDRA and ANISHAA look at each other nervously. ANISHAA nudges him.

NEELENDRA: I was afraid (**pause**) my family think Ive made a big mistake with my love marriage.

MYSTIC: Do not fear your dream. What have you asked for in recent prayers?

NEELENDRA: Well, I've asked Lord Krishna for an answer.

MYSTIC: The buffalo symbolises prayer and abundance, it says, 'Ask and it shall be given to you, be grateful for your blessings and you will receive.' The dream indicates you will be given what you have asked for.

The fire flares up. NEELENDRA looks away anxiously.

MYSTIC: But it is more complicated than that. In the dream it is you who are the mother, this represents a part of yourself you cannot face, yet you are already a father.

ANISHAA: What!

NEELENDRA: I don't understand, the dream, you said it's an answer to my prayer.

MYSTIC: It is an answer, but in unravelling this, it may not be the answer you seek. The dream speaks of your destiny, remember your kismet is larger than your own life. (**Pause**) I see that you want a son for your life to be fulfilled, it's as if you believe you must have a son to prove your worth to your family. (**Pause**) Be careful – where needs and desires cross the path of destiny only chaos will be found. What you love in your life may slip away from you.

NEELENDRA: (**whispers**) Cross the path of destiny, what is he talking about?

ANISHAA: (**whispers**) You know, if you fight against what's destined for you and want what can't be, then things will end up a mess.

NEELENDRA: What should I do now?

MYSTIC: Nothing, it has been done, I cannot interfere with your destiny, you know it deep within. The dream is a reflection of this, its significance will unravel with your life. I cannot tell you any more.

The flame in front of them flickers and dies. NEELENDRA lays some money down. ANISHAA and NEELENDRA get up and touch their foreheads as they leave.

ANISHAA: Is that really what you dreamt? I don't remember all that. And praying, I didn't know you were — (*praying for an answer*).

NEELENDRA: It sort of came back to me when he was asking the questions. What do you think's destined — (*for me?*)

ANISHAA: I cant be p . . . (*regnant*)

NEELENDRA: What did he mean about a son and being fulfilled?

ANISHAA strokes her belly.

Scene 2

Sixteen years later. ESHA (16), an Asian lad wearing a school tracksuit, tosses a football into the air and practises ball-skills in an alleyway. He counts with a rhyme as he does it.

ESHA: One for mummyji, one for daddyji, one for captainji, one for me. One for mummyji, one for daddyji, one for captainji, one for me.

ESHA becomes daring and practises across the railway level crossing, jumping out of the way just as he hears a train coming, it thunders past. ESHA watches it go and shouts in time to the train:

ESHA: One for me. One for me. One for me. One for me. (Laughs)

Scene 3

NEELENDRA (33, wearing a train-driver's uniform) sits at the kitchen table reading a newspaper. ANISHAA (32, wearing a green salwaar kameez) sprinkles some flour and then thumps some dough down onto the table in front of him.

ANISHAA: Do you want roti?

NEELENDRA answers from behind his newspaper.

NEELENDRA: Rice will do.

ANISHAA: I can make if you want.

NEELENDRA: Not bothered.

ANISHAA: Shall I wait for Esha then?

ANISHAA kneads the dough and starts to make rotia regardless. ESHA charges in carrying a Nike sports bag; he flings the bag under the table.

ESHA: Goal!

ANISHAA: Take it upstairs love, tea's nearly ready.

ESHA: What is it? I'm starving.

ANISHAA: Lamb.

ESHA sits at the table.

ANISHAA: Hello Esha, hello dad.

ESHA: He's reading.

NEELENDRA: Good game?

ESHA: All right, some of the lads are slacking off and it puts the drills out.

NEELENDRA: You've a couple of weeks yet. If they exhaust themselves now they'll have nothing left for the match. They're not all as obsessively fit as you.

ANISHAA continues to make rotia, laying them on the table beside NEELENDRA. NEELENDRA disappears behind the newspaper.

NEELENDRA: Help your mum.

ANISHAA: Just these rotia.

ESHA opens a chocolate bar. NEELENDRA puts down the paper.

NEELENDRA: Wait for your tea.

ANISHAA: Never mind, it's all that exercise. It won't be long love.

NEELENDRA: Oh he gets to spoil his tea, but I don't.

ESHA: Don't start you two, you'll give me indigestion.

ANISHAA gazes at the uncooked rotia and then at NEELENDRA. ESHA stuffs the chocolate bar into his mouth.

ANISHAA: How hungry are you?

NEELENDRA: Not very.

ANISHAA: Why didn't you say?

NEELENDRA: I said rice would do.

ANISHAA: I'm surprised you bother to stay for tea.

ESHA: (**mouth full of chocolate**) Stop it.

NEELENDRA: Don't you talk to your mum like that!

ANISHAA: Esha, don't talk with your mouth full.

ESHA: I'm talking to both of you.

ANISHAA: Well don't talk to your dad like that, he's had a hard day.

ANISHAA starts to push the rotia back into the dough.

ESHA: Yeah? He's not the only one 'round here whose days are shit.

ANISHAA: Esha!

NEELENDRA: Oh for god's sake Anishaa I'll eat them now they're made.

ESHA: Gotta dash.

NEELENDRA: Where do you think you're going?

ESHA: To the alley to practise.

NEELENDRA: No you're not. You can help your mum with the tea.

ANISHAA: It's all right, he's probably got homework to do.

ESHA: I don't.

NEELENDRA: Don't you? I can ring Mr Qureshi and check if Farooq has any. I'm sure his father doesn't allow him to roam the street at all hours.

ESHA: Dad! Don't embarrass me. Anyway he goes out when he wants.

ANISHAA: I'm sure he doesn't, he's a respectable — (*boy*)

NEELENDRA: Anishaa! I'll deal with this.

NEELENDRA bangs on the table with his fist, flour cascades onto the floor. ANISHAA jumps up and starts to clear it up.

NEELENDRA: Well you're not going out, you're out too much these days.

ESHA: I'm not staying here listening to your bollocks. You never let me have any freedom.

NEELENDRA: Watch your mouth.

ESHA bursts into tears and runs out.

NEELENDRA: You come back here.

ANISHAA: You're being too hard on him, he's a lot on with this training for the cup final. You know how seriously he takes his football.

NEELENDRA: Crying at his age? Just because he can't get his own way. He's too soft you mean. You've let him get away with too much.

ANISHAA: What does it matter whose fault it is?

Scene 4

ESHA wipes his face on his sweatshirt and tosses his football into the air. FAROOQ, (16) an Asian lad dressed in jeans and a shirt, watches from the side of the alleyway. ESHA doesn't notice him and starts his practice drill.

ESHA: One for mummyji, one for daddyji, one for captainji, one for me.

FAROOQ saunters over to ESHA.

FAROOQ: What's that shit you're saying?

ESHA kicks the football up and catches it in his hands.

ESHA: Just my training man.

FAROOQ: What's your mum and dad got to do with it?

ESHA: Nothing!

FAROOQ: I don't get it.

ESHA: That's the point. Neither do they. Help me, here.

ESHA lobs the football at FAROOQ. FAROOQ ducks out of the way, the football flies past him and rebounds off the wall.

ESHA: Catch. It's like living in a war zone.

FAROOQ: What d'you mean? They're no worse than mine.

ESHA: Don't want to talk about it.

FAROOQ throws the football back to ESHA.

FAROOQ: You're obsessive, man, this football lark drives me crazy.

ESHA: Yeah, but it makes you fast.

ESHA throws up the football and headers it.

ESHA: And fast makes you strong.

FAROOQ: I don't know why you play for the school. They just use you.

ESHA: So what! I love football.

FAROOQ: You lurve football! (**Laughs**) Don't be soft.

ESHA: So. You gotta love something sometime, might as well be this.

ESHA kicks the football hard towards FAROOQ. FAROOQ dodges out of the way.

FAROOQ: Watch it! Anyhow, why you training like a mad dog? I thought the final was in two weeks?

ESHA: It is. I gotta be as fit as I can 'cause I'm gonna win. I'm gonna score the winning goal.

FAROOQ: You're gonna win?

ESHA: We, we're gonna win the cup. There's a practice tomorrow night and I'm gonna be better than on form when the team gets selected.

FAROOQ: Really. (**Pause**) It's boring here, let's go hang out at Juicys.

ESHA: Nah. I don't want a kebab, I'm training.

FAROOQ playfully grabs ESHA and squeezes his thighs.

FAROOQ: You need the meat for your muscles.

ESHA: Yeah?

FAROOQ: You're getting boring.

ESHA grabs FAROOQ around the waist and squeezes him.

ESHA: And you're getting fat (**laughs**).

ESHA and FAROOQ look at each other, ESHA realises he's almost in an embrace with FAROOQ, he releases his grip, pulls away and grabs his belly in pain.

FAROOQ: What's wrong with you?

ESHA: Nought. (**Pause**) Something I ate.

FAROOQ looks concerned.

FAROOQ: All right man?

ESHA: Yeah 'course.

FAROOQ: Come on then. We can hang out with girls, play pinball.

ESHA: There's too many fights. You'll get into trouble again.

FAROOQ: All right, finish up, it's getting dark, bloody gay.

ESHA: I can see in the dark and I'm too tough to be a gay.

FAROOQ: Well you're gonna get called that shit unless you lose your virginity soon.

ESHA: No way man! It takes away from your fitness.

FAROOQ: I'm gonna get you lined up for after the match.

ESHA starts to header the ball.

ESHA: If you can find anyone I fancy.

FAROOQ: Yes! I'm off to Juicys to line someone up now.

ESHA: After the final.

FAROOQ: She can come to the match. You better win.

ESHA: Don't worry.

FAROOQ starts to leave.

FAROOQ: That'll get her going seeing your thunderous thighs pounding up the midfield like a streak of lightning (**laughs**). And we'd better get your outfit sorted out. No one's going to go for you in that tracksuit.

ESHA: Let's see if you can find someone I fancy first.

FAROOQ: I will.

FAROOQ disappears into the darkness of the evening. ESHA headers the football.

ESHA: She's got to be better than football or I'm not even looking once.

ESHA misses the return and the football rolls away from him.

ESHA: Shit!

ESHA grips his belly and peers into the darkness looking for the football.

Scene 5

ANISHAA stands in front of a shrine, her feet are bare, her duputta covers her head. ANISHAA lights incense and a candle, places them on the shrine and puts her hands together in prayer.

ANISHAA: (**Sings**) Radha Govinder, Radha Govinder, Radha Govinder. Om Shanti, Shanti, Shanti, Om. (**Pause**) One day of harmony, just one day.

ANISHAA blows out the candle. ESHA enters the kitchen carrying his Nike sports bag. ESHA suddenly stops in his tracks, drops his bag and grips his belly.

ESHA: (groans).

ANISHAA enters the kitchen, her duputta is over her shoulders and she has an apron on.

ANISHAA: Esha? You're home early. What's up?

ESHA: I've got pains in here.

ESHA points to his belly. ANISHAA approaches ESHA, he steps back.

ANISHAA: In your stomach?

ESHA points to his belly again.

ESHA: I want it to go away.

ANISHAA: What about an ice-pack?

ESHA: It's not that sort of pain.

ANISHAA: Have you eaten something to upset it?

ESHA shakes his head no.

ANISHAA: You've not been eating those greasy kebabs again?

ESHA: No, it's not something I've eaten. It's, um, you know.

ESHA grips his stomach.

ANISHAA: What? I don't know. Men are such babies when they get hurt. You've probably been training too hard. You go upstairs and lie down and it'll probably ease off. Here, give me your — (*bag*)

ANISHAA reaches for his bag.

ESHA: I'll do it.

ANISHAA: And I'll wash your kit for — (*tomorrow night*).

ESHA: Stop fussing me.

ANISHAA: One minute you want help, the next I'm fussing. I can't win with you. (**Laughs**) Anyway, you've never used the washing machine before now, so I can't see you doing your kit yourself.

ANISHAA tries to prise the bag from his hands. ESHA pulls it away.

ESHA: Mum! I said I'll do it.

ANISHAA: Don't get nasty like that. You sound just like your father.

ANISHAA grabs the sports bag, unzips it and empties ESHA's football strip onto the table. ANISHAA picks up his white shorts, they are stained in blood. ESHA looks down at his feet.

ANISHAA: Oh!

ANISHAA tries to stuff the shorts back in the bag. ANISHAA looks away.

ESHA: Mum.

ANISHAA: Don't worry, I won't tell your father, you know how he's always going on about having to buy you new clothes. They just need a soak, that's all.

ESHA hauls them out and holds them up.

ANISHAA: It's okay. They'll still be ready for tomorrow.

ESHA: It's not a cut.

ANISHAA: Maybe, you didn't feel it. You go upstairs and clean up, there's some Dettol in the bathroom.

ESHA: But.

ANISHAA: Come on. You're a big boy now. You know what to do. I can't be mopping up your scratches and scrapes forever.

ANISHAA puts the shorts back in the bag and zips it up.

ANISHAA: There's a packet of aspirin in the bathroom cabinet.

ESHA: I want to win.

ANISHAA: Win?

ESHA: The cup.

ANISHAA: Of course you will. Come on, get yourself cleaned up before your dad comes home.

ANISHAA and ESHA look at each other.

Scene 6

It is sunny. ESHA sits on the railway level crossing and yawns as he reads a copy of *Sugar*, a girls' magazine.

ESHA: How can anyone read this shit? What a load of bollocks. 'Dear Rebecca, my boyfriend wants me to kiss him but he's got spots and bad breath, what can I do? From Wendy.' 'Dear Wendy if you really want to kiss him then you'll find a way to help him solve his problems. Try talking to him about a mouthwash and some facial scrub. Yours Truly, Rebecca.' What does the silly tart want to kiss him for anyhow, she might catch something.

ESHA continues to scan the magazine, pointing at the pages.

ESHA: I'm never going to wear that shit on my face or those clothes.

ESHA tears a page from the magazine, he reads from it.

ESHA: Aries. Today you'll see somewhere you haven't been before. There are always two sides, look for the answer in more than one place.

ESHA shrugs his shoulders, then folds the page up and puts it in his pocket.

ESHA: It's all made up anyway.

ESHA turns the page of the magazine.

ESHA: It's crap this. It doesn't tell me what to do now. Where's my problem on the Dear Rebecca page? It isn't there is it?

ESHA pretends to write.

ESHA: Dear Rebecca, yesterday I started my (**pause**) bled all over my football shorts, I had to leave football training early and I could barely walk home with the pain. P.S. I'm a boy. From Confused of Mirfield. Dear Confused, stop taking the piss, you can't be a boy and have your period.

ESHA shuts the magazine.

ESHA: No, that's no good. (**Pause**) Dear Confused, how could you end up in that position? You better talk it through with your mother because I can assure you boys don't have periods.

ESHA throws the magazine down, lies back and shuts his eyes.

ESHA: I know. When I was five she told me mirrors were bad and never to look in one, and when I said I wanted to be a footballer she bought me my first strip. And by the time I knew what being a boy meant, it was too late.

ESHA runs his hand down his body.

ESHA: Why does it have to change now? I can't become someone I'm not, never have been. (**Pause**) Why hasn't anyone noticed? Hid it too well, I suppose; baggy clothes, bandages, jockstraps, and not allowing anyone near my clothed body, let alone kiss me.

ESHA feels his lips with his fingers.

ESHA: I act like a son, speak like a son, perform like a son. (**Pause**) I am their son.

FAROOQ runs over to ESHA and balances on the railway lines. ESHA wakes and is startled.

FAROOQ: There you are. Why've you not been at school today?

ESHA: Er, faking it, needed time out.

FAROOQ: Yeah? Wicked! But you're missing your sacred training.

ESHA: Pulled a muscle.

FAROOQ: Where?

ESHA: Nowhere man.

FAROOQ: Nowhere?

ESHA: Groin strain.

FAROOQ: Oh, there is life down there then.

ESHA: How was school?

FAROOQ: Boring. What you been doing all day?

ESHA: Sitting here.

FAROOQ: Boring.

FAROOQ listens.

FAROOQ: Get up. The 4.19's due.

ESHA: It's my dad's, he'll stop when he sees me.

FAROOQ: He can't see you. Get up idiot!

FAROOQ leaps off the tracks. ESHA waits until the last minute, the sound of the train grows louder, ESHA rolls off the track just in time.

ESHA: Chicken.

FAROOQ: If I'm a chicken then you're a chicken brain. What are you trying to prove?

ESHA: Not trying to prove anything. What d'you mean?

FAROOQ picks up the magazine.

FAROOQ: *Sugar*! Whose is this?

ESHA: Dunno, it was lying here.

FAROOQ: Wanna see if there's anything tasty in it?

ESHA: It's stupid girlie stuff.

FAROOQ: You've probably checked it out, look the pages are stuck together.

ESHA: Yeah, I did, they're all ugly.

FAROOQ opens the magazine.

FAROOQ: She's a bit of all right, what about her?

FAROOQ shows ESHA the magazine.

ESHA: Not my type.

FAROOQ: Better start thinking about it before the match.

ESHA: Is she yours?

FAROOQ: What?

ESHA: You know, type?

FAROOQ: She's good looking, but you know Asian girls are more my style.

ESHA: Well why do you hang round with that tart Susan if she's not your type?

FAROOQ: She's a laugh and she's okay looking, but not stunning like Shanaz. If I saw Shanaz in a sari I think I'd pass out with longing.

ESHA looks down at his tracksuit.

FAROOQ: Talking of types, let's get your criteria worked out.

ESHA flicks through the pages of the magazine.

ESHA: How about, if we win the final then I don't bother with lasses an' that shit.

FAROOQ: You need to lighten up. (**Pause**) I'm not letting you get out of it that easily, you're bound to win. What's the problem?

ESHA: There's no fit babes around here.

FAROOQ: There's loads. Your hormones aren't working.

ESHA: (**startled**) What do you mean?

FAROOQ: You're supposed to get a hard-on when you look at a babe.

ESHA: I do, if she's fit!

FAROOQ: I'm gonna find you a real stunner, that'll get your mechanics working.

ESHA: I'll believe it when I see it.

FAROOQ: You will.

ESHA gets up.

ESHA: Shit! It's me mum.

FAROOQ: What's the problem?

ESHA: She's on me back, that's what.

FAROOQ: Later man.

ESHA runs off. ANISHAA strides over to FAROOQ. FAROOQ hides the magazine behind his back.

ANISHAA: Hello Farooq.

FAROOQ: Hello auntieji.

ANISHAA: Have you seen Esha?

FAROOQ: No, I mean at school, but he, er, stayed late as usual.

ANISHAA: We've hardly seen him the last few days. His dad encourages all this training, but he's the first to complain when Esha gets a bad grade at school. I'm worried about him, it can't be good for you every night.

FAROOQ: Dunno, never done much training.

ANISHAA: Have you noticed, I mean, is he okay?

FAROOQ: Fine, well he strained a muscle an' he was — (*doubled up*)

ANISHAA: A muscle, and he still went to training?

FAROOQ: You know what he's like, he doesn't know when to stop.

ANISHAA: Yes, he's got to do everything his own way.

FAROOQ: The coach won't let him play if he's injured though.

ANISHAA: I suppose.

FAROOQ: He'll be all right, he just wants to win this match really badly, that's all he thinks about. I can't get him to come to Ju — (icys)

ANISHAA starts to walk away.

ANISHAA: What?

FAROOQ: Think about anything else either.

ANISHAA: I must go, I've got a lot on.

FAROOQ: You'll get him back, Mrs Annand, when it's all over.

Scene 7

ANISHAA lights incense and a candle on her shrine in the kitchen. She closes her eyes and places her hands together in prayer, then she turns away from her shrine.

ANISHAA: Lord Krishna, hear my prayer, hear my small voice in the universe that you dwell in. If only my life was simple, if only that I need ask for sun in the morning, moon at night, but it is not so. The truth I wanted has become a lie and I can't hide from it any more. When I stared into his eyes, when I, I had only love in my thoughts.

ESHA stands in front of a mirror, he takes a red kameez and holds it up to himself, he is shocked and lets it slide from his fingers to the floor. He pushes up his sleeves and looks at his muscly arms in the mirror, then rolls them down again.

ANISHAA: Lord Krishna remember you named a son for me and you have watched him grow with my daily prayer. You know from watching that he has not the body of a son and blossoms sweetly like any woman. I have tried to live not in darkness but in light, attempted to seek knowledge and turn from ignorance and evil. I have abided by my duties as a wife and mother, always remembering that I am a daughter.

At the mirror ESHA slowly picks up the kameez and looks again at his image. He tries the kameez on over his tracksuit and drapes the duputta over his head. ESHA takes the duputta off his head, flings it around his shoulders and smiles at his reflection in the mirror.

ANISHAA: I do not know why I am given this kismet but I need an answer if I am to carry on struggling with my meagre life. You have held up mountains, but my burden is larger than any mountain. Hear me Lord Krishna, answer my prayer, make my life whole again.

ANISHAA's head leans to one side as if she's dreaming. ESHA, dressed in the red salwaar kameez and duputta, walks into the kitchen. He stops in his tracks when he sees his mum and tries to sneak out. ANISHAA turns around and looks surprised, she starts to get up.

ANISHAA: Who's that? Esha? It can't be. Khon? Tum? Kaahini?

ANISHAA drops to her knees. ESHA freezes. ANISHAA clasps her hands in prayer and squeezes her eyes shut tight.

ANISHAA: Lord Krishna thank you, you've given me back my daughter. Thank you, thank you.

ESHA scarpers. ANISHAA opens her eyes.

ANISHAA: No, don't take her, don't take her from me, not again.

ANISHA's head drops in her hands and she starts to sob gently.

ESHA, dressed in the red salwaar kameez and duputta, runs across the alleyway. He crashes into **FAROOQ** coming in the other direction. **FAROOQ** eyes him intently. **ESHA** avoids **FAROOQ**'s gaze by hiding behind his duputta.

ESHA: I was just . . . (*I can't explain*)

FAROOQ: What?

ESHA: I don't want you to get it wrong.

FAROOQ: Eh?

ESHA stands awkwardly in the salwaar kameez and adjusts his duputta.

FAROOQ: Sorry, have I met you before?

ESHA: No, my mistake.

FAROOQ: I don't mind. What's your name then?

ESHA looks at FAROOQ from under the duputta.

ESHA: Er, Kaahini.

FAROOQ: That's an unusual name.

KAAHINI/ESHA: I am unusual!

FAROOQ: What d'you mean?

KAAHINI/ESHA: I'll tell you another day.

FAROOQ: Hey, do you like kebabs?

KAAHINI/ESHA: They're all right. What's it to you?

FAROOQ: Hey, wanna come to Juicys? It's just up the next street.

KAAHINI/ESHA tries to look at FAROOQ from under the duputta. She bites her lip.

KAAHINI/ESHA: No.

FAROOQ: I haven't seen you around here. Been to Juicys? It's wicked!

KAAHINI/ESHA: No. Um, I'm not allowed.

FAROOQ: No one'll know.

KAAHINI/ESHA: Anyway, I can't go dressed up like this.

FAROOQ: Why not? It's in fashion to wear 'Asian' just now. Half the girls who hang round Juicys wear it, and that's just the white girls (**laughs**).

KAAHINI/ESHA: Do they?

FAROOQ: Yeah. Come on, I'll treat you to a double shish with loads of chilli sauce.

KAAHINI/ESHA: Just for half an hour, (**pause**) and if I see anyone I know I'm off.

FAROOQ tries to walk close to KAAHINI/ESHA, she moves away.

KAAHINI/ESHA: What's your name then?

FAROOQ: Farooq.

KAAHINI/ESHA: Farooq. What does it mean?

FAROOQ: Dunno. What does yours mean?

KAAHINI/ESHA: Don't know.

FAROOQ: You're not at my school are you?

KAAHINI/ESHA: No, anyway I've left.

FAROOQ: So you, er, haven't heard of me?

KAAHINI/ESHA: No. I said I got it wrong!

FAROOQ: (**to himself**) Fish are biting!

KAAHINI/ESHA: What?

FAROOQ: Nothing. You working?

KAAHINI/ESHA: No.

FAROOQ grabs KAAHINI/ESHA's left hand and looks at her fingers, she tries to pull away, FAROOQ looks at her.

FAROOQ: Just checking you're not married.

KAAHINI/ESHA: (**laughs**) Do you think I'd come to a kebab shop with you if I was?

FAROOQ: No, suppose not. So how old are you?

KAAHINI/ESHA: Sixteen.

KAAHINI/ESHA tries to free her hand, FAROOQ doesn't let go, KAAHINI/ESHA pulls away.

KAAHINI/ESHA: You?

FAROOQ: Sixteen, sweet sixteen and never been.

FAROOQ kisses KAAHINI/ESHA on the hand, she pulls away and runs off. FAROOQ starts after her.

FAROOQ: Kaahini, wait! I'm not, it's not.

FAROOQ stops in his tracks.

FAROOQ: Shit!

FAROOQ slumps on the wall and practices his kissing technique on the back of his hand. NEELENDRA approaches on his way home from work.

NEELENDRA: Missing your friend?

FAROOQ: What! Oh, hello Mr Annand. If you see Esha, tell him I'm waiting for him.

NEELENDRA: That's what I was saying, I think he's training late tonight. Didn't he tell you?

FAROOQ: No, he said something about a strained muscle yesterday.

NEELENDRA: Did he? Seemed fit enough to me. Want to come home and wait?

FAROOQ: Better get off.

NEELENDRA: Auntie's made some khanna. Hungry?

FAROOQ: Nah, not really. I mean no thank you.

NEELENDRA: I thought boys were hungry all the time, our Esha eats like there's no tomorrow.

FAROOQ: I know, I've seen him eat a double shish kebab with double chilli.

NEELENDRA: Have you now. Not recently though?

FAROOQ: Oh no, that was ages ago, before he started training.

NEELENDRA: You play any sport these days?

FAROOQ: Me? Only running I do is after lasses. (**Pause**) It's a joke, you know me, I couldn't run for a bus. I missed one going into town last week.

NEELENDRA: It's not that I think you should disregard girls, but running after them, there's a time for that Farooq.

FAROOQ: Yeah and it's my uncle who'll do the running, with his orange beard flapping behind him.

NEELENDRA: And so he should. Who d'you think you're going to find here on the streets to marry? You'd make a good son-in-law so don't you mess things up for yourself.

NEELENDRA puts his arm around FAROOQ in a fatherly way and then starts to go.

FAROOQ: Mr Annand, you know when you told me before, about love and that.

NEELENDRA stops in his tracks.

FAROOQ: Well, what if you meet a great girl you want to marry, what do you do then?

NEELENDRA turns FAROOQ to face him, man to man.

NEELENDRA: Depends on who it is I suppose. (**Pause**) Marriages are built on trust, you can't be whimsical about who you marry, it's for life. (**Pause**) Have you, are you in any trouble Farooq?

FAROOQ: No, no, of course not. I meant, say, you met someone and that.

NEELENDRA: (**suspicious**) What about Esha?

FAROOQ: What about him?

NEELENDRA: Is there something to tell about Esha, that he can't tell me for some reason?

FAROOQ: Him! He's not interested in girls, too busy running after a football.

NEELENDRA: Hmm, always training that boy, not much time for being boyish, eh Farooq?

NEELENDRA slaps FAROOQ on the back, FAROOQ stumbles and nearly falls.

FAROOQ: But say you — (*wanted to ask a girl*)

NEELENDRA: Do you think they'll win the cup?

FAROOQ: With a striker like Esha, definitely.

NEELENDRA: Yes, he needs to think wider than, football now. He's got to think about his future.

NEELENDRA pats the wall and they sit down.

FAROOQ: So — (*if you wanted*)

NEELENDRA: How's your studies?

FAROOQ: Fine.

NEELENDRA: Applied to university?

FAROOQ: No, well, maybe. My dad wants me to manage his business.

NEELENDRA: Stationery, well there's always demand for that.

FAROOQ: Boring, going nowhere. It is stationary.

NEELENDRA: Well then, there's a challenge. You could turn it around, take it somewhere couldn't you?

FAROOQ: Suppose so.

NEELENDRA: Why don't I talk to your father about a degree in Business Studies?

FAROOQ: I dunno, he's not into education an' that sh . . .

NEELENDRA: Think about it. Better go for my roti or it will be cold on the table. (**Pause**) Sure you don't want — (some?)

FAROOQ: No, tell Esha.

NEELENDRA: Yes.

FAROOQ: Oh nothing.

Scene 8

ESHA dribbles the football down the alleyway. FAROOQ approaches ESHA, he has a ghetto-blaster on his shoulder, 'Kizmet', Talvin Singh, blasts out.

FAROOQ: (**shouts**) Esha man. Where've you been? I've been looking for you all over. What happened to you yesterday?

FAROOQ puts the ghetto-blaster down. He runs up and tackles ESHA, winning the ball easily, he dribbles it away from ESHA and kicks it hard at the wall.

FAROOQ: Goal! (**Pause**) Shit. What's wrong with you? You've never let me win a tackle.

ESHA switches the ghetto-blaster off.

ESHA: Nought.

FAROOQ: Training going all right?

ESHA: Under pressure.

FAROOQ: What d'you mean?

ESHA: You know, my dad going on about university again. He kept me in last night studying after school and I er, missed training.

FAROOQ: Your dad? I saw him last night and he said you were training.

ESHA: Yeah, I mean he got my mum to keep me in. He doesn't remember, can't tell the sun from the moon when he's on nights.

FAROOQ: Well that was last night, you're out tonight aren't you?

Kaahini

ESHA: Yeah, but he says I've got to choose. Remember last year when he filled in my choices for GCSEs. He handed me back the paper and said 'These are your best choices.' What does he bloody know about choice?

FAROOQ: Do the degree, keep them happy, then you can do what you want. It'll give you some bargaining power.

ESHA: Whose side you on man?

FAROOQ: Touchy!

ESHA: I want to do what I want now. I gotta play footie now, while I'm young and fit.

FAROOQ: It doesn't work like that. At least your choice is better than mine. I get to work in my old man's stationery shop.

ESHA: Don't you want to run the shop?

FAROOQ: Spend my life looking at dusty piles of Bic biros. No thanks. (**Pause**) Anyway, you can play footie at university. I might do business studies.

ESHA: You? Since when did you want to study? Anyway, I don't want to do banking, I want to be a professional footballer.

FAROOQ: The course doesn't matter, it's the quality of the women at the university that counts.

ESHA: You've got a one track mind.

FAROOQ: So have you. Anyway, guess what.

ESHA: What? Don't tell me, you scored.

FAROOQ: Yeah, and it's Farooq one, Esha nil.

ESHA: Come on then, bore me with the details.

FAROOQ: Don't be like that.

FAROOQ gestures with his hands.

FAROOQ: She's got beautiful almond eyes and she was wearing a wicked little red salwaar kameez, a real Asian lass.

ESHA is panicked and looks at his feet.

ESHA: I thought you're only into white girls.

FAROOQ: Yeah, just to mess around with. Kaahini's different.

ESHA: Kaahini! (**Pause**) Shit man, what kind of a name is that?

FAROOQ: I dunno, it's not Muslim.

ESHA: What the fuck do you think you're playing at?

FAROOQ: I'm in lurve.

ESHA is shocked and turns away.

ESHA: You wouldn't know what that shit was if it hit you between the eyes.

FAROOQ: Neither would you. Anyway it has. She's the business.

ESHA: What's going on with you two then?

FAROOQ: Hang on, I haven't even filled you in yet.

ESHA: Get on with it. Is she fit?

FAROOQ: Thought you weren't interested in my love life.

FAROOQ and ESHA look at each other, FAROOQ adopts a defiant pose.

FAROOQ: Yeah she's gorgeous, seriously feminine.

ESHA: What do you like most about her?

FAROOQ: What you want to know all this for, fancy a bit yourself eh? Better watch what I say in front of you.

ESHA: I'm yer friend void-brain! (**Pause**) Are you really in love?

FAROOQ: Love at first sight Esha man.

ESHA: Does she know you love her?

FAROOQ: 'Course not man, you don't tell them your feelings otherwise they get the upper hand.

ESHA: It's just a game to you.

ESHA scoops up the football irritably.

ESHA: If you don't mind I've got a match to win.

FAROOQ: Come on man. Maybe she's got a friend, we could have a foursome.

ESHA: I've no time for a girlfriend. After the final it's hard graft for me on the studying front.

FAROOQ: He'll let you out at weekends.

ESHA: Anyway, I told you, there's no one fit.

FAROOQ: And I promised to line you up after the game.

ESHA: Don't bother.

FAROOQ: You said.

ESHA: I've changed my mind.

FAROOQ: Well, if you don't want one, aren't you happy for me?

ESHA: Ecstatic.

FAROOQ: Piss off then. I find the girl of my dreams and you couldn't care less.

ESHA: She's just a girl.

FAROOQ: Not an ordinary girl, she's something special.

ESHA: You don't even know her.

FAROOQ: I don't need to. I can feel it.

ESHA: Where? In your balls?

ESHA makes a thrusting gesture with his hips.

FAROOQ: Piss off. I haven't touched her.

ESHA: Haven't you?

FAROOQ: I swear, you're acting weird man. What's going on?

ESHA: **(interrupts)** Well what do you love about her then?

FAROOQ: She's different, **(pause)** not like other girls I've met. She's sussed, knows what she wants. Satisfied now?

ESHA: That's nice for you.

FAROOQ: You're jealous, that's what's wrong with you.

ESHA: No I'm not. I'm happy for you man. When you seeing her again?

FAROOQ: Didn't make a date, I'll just catch her around.

ESHA: So how do you know she's interested?

FAROOQ: She is, I could tell the way she looked at me.

ESHA: How did she look at you?

FAROOQ: Esha man, you've got a lot to learn. **(Pause)** She'll be back. End of conversation.

ESHA: Where does she live?

FAROOQ: I dunno!

ESHA: You don't know much about this girl you love.

FAROOQ: That's it, I'm off, I've had enough of this interrogation, you're bang out of order.

FAROOQ starts to go.

FAROOQ: I'm gonna go and find Kaahini.

ESHA: Don't go. Help me do some tactics.

FAROOQ: You're not interested in me, so I couldn't care less about your stupid footie.

ESHA: I am. We can like different things.

FAROOQ: Yeah, whatever. See you around.

FAROOQ switches on the ghetto-blaster, it nearly drowns ESHA out.

ESHA: Come on man, I thought we were friends, you gonna let a girl come between us?

Scene 9

ANISHAA stands over the kitchen table rolling rotia, NEELENDRA stands behind her.

ANISHAA: I don't want to go to the wedding, I'm not in the mood.

NEELENDRA: Come on Nisha.

ANISHAA: I can't go, I've nothing to wear.

NEELENDRA: What about that new red salwaar kameez I bought for you on our anniversary?

ANISHAA: I can't find it.

NEELENDRA: I saw it in your wardrobe the other day.

ANISHAA: It's not there, I don't want to wear red.

NEELENDRA: It's your favourite colour. You'll enjoy it when you get there, meeting up for a gossip with your friends.

ANISHAA: I don't feel like talking to anyone, I can't.

NEELENDRA: What's wrong?

ANISHAA: Nothing.

NEELENDRA: (**laughs**) There is, you've been moody all week.

ANISHAA turns to face NEELENDRA, she has a roti in her hands.

ANISHAA: (**shouts**) I have not been moody.

ANISHAA throws the roti across the table.

NEELENDRA: Anishaa, you're getting hysterical again.

ANISHAA: (**shouts**) I am not getting hysterical. Every time I raise my voice I'm hysterical and every time I'm a little down in the dumps I'm depressed.

NEELENDRA: I've had to put up with your moods for sixteen years.

ANISHAA: Moods! I've lived in this darkness because of you.

NEELENDRA: Because of me? It's all in your head if you ask me Anishaa.

ANISHAA: Exactly. Running away from our families, because of love, having to live here in this (**pause**) country. How do you think that made me feel?

NEELENDRA: We didn't run away, it was your idea to come to England for god's sake.

ANISHAA: You wanted to as much as me.

NEELENDRA: Yes, and we said five years to make some money, and look at us now.

ANISHAA: Don't start all that again, you know we've stayed so that our son gets a better education.

NEELENDRA: Its not just about you Anishaa. I've made sacrifices too remember (**pause**) – never did my bank exams. What's done is done, you can't live in the past forever.

NEELENDRA reaches out to touch ANISHAA's face, she glares at him angrily.

NEELENDRA: We were young, we both gave up things. (**Pause**) Homesick again, is this what's troubling you? We've coped before. Let's go to the wedding, it'll cheer you up.

ANISHAA pushes his hand out of the way.

ANISHAA: You, you're what's troubling me. You and your blinkered vision. I don't call shutting off from everything coping. (**Pause**) You just can't change nature.

NEELENDRA turns away.

ANISHAA: I was praying, thought it was a vision, I saw an Asian girl, but it was E — (*sha*).

NEELENDRA: I hope for Esha's sake you didn't see a girl in this house.

ESHA arrives home, but stops when he hears his parents arguing. He watches and listens from a distance.

NEELENDRA: Because that's all we need, a girl to bring the family name down.

ANISHAA: (**sobbing**) I, I saw my dau — (*ghter*).

NEELENDRA: If you're going to start all that wanting a daughter I'm not staying around for it. We have a son and that's it. (**Pause**) You know you can't have any more children. Your prayers have taken you into some fantasy world.

ESHA hears this and storms in.

ANISHAA: What about our son's future? He can't — (*get married*).

ESHA: Mum, dad? What's going on?

NEELENDRA: Ask her, she's ranting on about the past again.

ANISHAA continues to sob quietly.

ESHA: Mum?

ANISHAA: He won't listen to me, can't see, tell him Esha, tell him.

ESHA: Can't see what?

ANISHAA: Esha, please.

ESHA looks blankly at ANISHAA. ANISHAA runs out.

NEELENDRA: Tell me what? Esha, have you got a girl into trouble or something? Your mum said something about an Asian girl.

ESHA: Dad!

NEELENDRA: I know you probably can't talk to her, she's too sensitive, but I need to you come clean with me son.

ESHA: There's nothing to come clean about man.

NEELENDRA: Come on.

ESHA: I don't know what she means.

ESHA shrugs his shoulders and starts to leave.

NEELENDRA: Where do you think you're going?

ESHA: Training.

NEELENDRA: I thought you were injured?

ESHA: Oh that, it's fine, just needed an ice-pack.

ESHA starts to leave, NEELENDRA pulls him back by the arm.

NEELENDRA: Just a minute.

ESHA: Come on dad.

ESHA tries to pull away. NEELENDRA turns ESHA to face him.

ESHA: I can't let the team down. There's only a few training days left before the match.

NEELENDRA: Let me see . . . (*my boy*).

NEELENDRA admires his son and hands ESHA his Nike bag.

NEELENDRA: You won't get far without this.

ESHA: Ta dad. You'll see, we're gonna win.

ESHA sprints off.

NEELENDRA: Win? Winning, that's all I hear from him, have I brought him up like this? To be full of the ambition my father fed me with morning and night, and still I couldn't be who he wanted me to be. (**Pause**) Son, there's more to life than winning, don't forget to live, otherwise you'll end up like your father, bitter and sad and always trying to please a broken woman.

Scene 10

KAAHINI/ESHA, dressed in the red salwaar kameez and duputta, stands in front of a mirror, puts lipstick on and admires her reflection. KAAHINI/ESHA strolls into the alleyway and stuffs her Nike bag behind the wall.

FAROOQ walks down the alleyway and spots KAAHINI/ESHA. FAROOQ creeps up behind her and puts his hands over her eyes. KAAHINI/ESHA pulls FAROOQ's hands away and then throws him on the ground.

KAAHINI/ESHA: Farooq!

FAROOQ gets up, rubbing his wrist.

FAROOQ: Kaahini! You nearly snapped my wrist off.

KAAHINI/ESHA: Sorry, don't know my own strength (**laughs**).

FAROOQ: Yeah. (**Pause**) You're strong for a girl!

KAAHINI/ESHA: Oh, I, um, do fitness.

FAROOQ: Where did you learn to do that throw?

KAAHINI/ESHA: At the (**pause**) youthie, I did a self defence course for, er, girls.

FAROOQ: Oh. (**Pause**) What you doing — (*here?*)

KAAHINI/ESHA: Don't you want to see me?

FAROOQ: I wasn't expecting you, I'm waiting for my mate.

KAAHINI/ESHA: I'll get off then.

KAAHINI/ESHA starts to leave.

FAROOQ: No! He's late. I mean, Id like you to stay.

KAAHINI/ESHA looks away and smirks.

FAROOQ: I've been thinking about you ever since we met, it's just that I didn't expect to see you again after you ran off. What happened?

KAAHINI/ESHA: You, um, took me by surprise.

FAROOQ: I've missed you.

KAAHINI/ESHA: Don't be soft m . . . (*an*), you don't even know me.

FAROOQ: Well I've missed what I know of you. Anyway, you're not getting out of it this time, when Esha gets here we can go to Juicys.

KAAHINI/ESHA: I've just eaten.

FAROOQ: Don't you want to see me?

KAAHINI/ESHA: Why d'you think I'm here!

FAROOQ: 'Cause you like me?

KAAHINI/ESHA: Yeah.

FAROOQ: Have you had a boyfriend before?

KAAHINI/ESHA: No, but I've er, read about boys.

FAROOQ: You can't believe the rubbish in magazines, it's all made up you know.

KAAHINI/ESHA: So how many girlfriends have you had?

FAROOQ: You're my first.

KAAHINI/ESHA: I can't believe a good-looking guy like you has been single all his life.

FAROOQ: Saving myself for you.

KAAHINI/ESHA: Yeah right.

FAROOQ: Who you been listening to?

KAAHINI/ESHA: No one, what d'you mean?

FAROOQ: It doesn't matter. So I'm your first?

KAAHINI/ESHA: First what?

FAROOQ: Boyfriend.

KAAHINI/ESHA: Suppose.

FAROOQ: You are my girlfriend aren't you?

KAAHINI/ESHA: Maybe. What's he like this mate of yours?

FAROOQ: Who?

KAAHINI/ESHA: Your best mate.

FAROOQ: Okay, cool. Bit of a sod sometimes though, especially when he can't get his own way.

KAAHINI/ESHA: What does he do?

FAROOQ: He's at school with me.

KAAHINI/ESHA: No, I mean what does he do when he can't get his own way?

FAROOQ: Tries to sit on me until I give in, but I'm much stronger than him, could throw him off any day.

KAAHINI/ESHA: Could you?

FAROOQ: Yeah. He's good at football, he's gonna be famous.

KAAHINI/ESHA: Yeah?

FAROOQ: Plays for the school team, puts up with a lot of racist shit but he's fast man, real fast.

KAAHINI/ESHA looks away.

KAAHINI/ESHA: Fast, but not strong.

FAROOQ: Where the hell is he? He's supposed to be here.

KAAHINI/ESHA: He's probably not coming, lets go to Juicys. Come on.

FAROOQ: Nah, I gotta wait for him, its important, I can't deff him out. Just stick around for eighty seconds. Thought you'd eaten?

KAAHINI/ESHA: I'm hungry now.

FAROOQ: I promise we'll go when he gets here. Have you got a mate for him, he's too busy playing footie to get a girlfriend an' that.

KAAHINI/ESHA: I'm not into all that fixing up an' shit. People meet when people meet, it's their kismet.

FAROOQ: Is this our kismet?

KAAHINI/ESHA: Maybe.

FAROOQ: You're cool.

KAAHINI/ESHA: Am I?

FAROOQ: Yeah, never met a girl like you before.

KAAHINI/ESHA: So who comes first, your girl or your mate?

FAROOQ: Dunno, your mates are important.

KAAHINI/ESHA sits down on the wall.

KAAHINI/ESHA: Let's not talk about him any more.

FAROOQ: You're like Esha in a way.

KAAHINI/ESHA: What do you mean?

FAROOQ: Oh it's nothing.

KAAHINI/ESHA: I gotta go.

FAROOQ: Stay.

KAAHINI/ESHA: I can't.

FAROOQ: Do you want to see me again?

KAAHINI/ESHA: Yeah.

FAROOQ puts his arm around KAAHINI/ESHA. KAAHINI/ESHA tries to move away.

FAROOQ: I thought you said you wanted to see me.

KAAHINI/ESHA: Yeah, well don't push it.

KAAHINI/ESHA gets off the wall.

KAAHINI/ESHA: See ya.

FAROOQ: You've only just got here.

KAAHINI/ESHA strides off. FAROOQ grabs the Nike bag from behind the wall and starts to follow her.

FAROOQ: Wait!

KAAHINI/ESHA: What you playing at?

FAROOQ: You forgot your bag. Meet me in Juicys at eight tonight.

KAAHINI/ESHA: Maybe.

KAAHINI/ESHA leaps onto the wall and runs along the length of it fearlessly. FAROOQ watches her go.

   FAROOQ walks to the end of the alleyway eyeing his reflection in the side of an old railway carriage. He does two or three dance steps and then spins around three times chanting:

Kaahini

FAROOQ: She loves me,
   loves me not,
   loves me,
   loves me not,
   she loves me.

FAROOQ spins around again, sits on the wall and chomps on a Snickers. ESHA leaps over the wall.

FAROOQ: Where've you been? I've been waiting man, and you've just missed Kaahini.

ESHA: Kept in studying.

FAROOQ: You're not avoiding me then?

ESHA: Nah man, it's cool.

FAROOQ: Touch, nice. You gotta sneak out or something, it's getting bad.

ESHA: You're telling me, if I don't make training this week I'll be out of the team.

ESHA traces some graffiti on the wall with his finger.

ESHA: Sharon loves Paul, Ellie loves Simon, Farooq loves Kaahini.

FAROOQ: What? Where does it say that?

ESHA: It doesn't, I was just messing.

FAROOQ: Shit, how many Farooqs do you know around here? I'd be in major trouble if anyone wrote that shit about me.

ESHA: Your dad's not going to come around here reading walls.

FAROOQ: Yeah but some nosy cousin might.

ESHA: They wouldn't tell your dad.

FAROOQ: Wouldn't they? They can't wait to have some gossip about me cause they're pissed off I get more freedom than them. They're just waiting.

ESHA: What would your dad do?

FAROOQ: Ground me, for starters.

ESHA: He never seems strict an' that shit.

FAROOQ: He's too busy working and hanging with his cronies to bother much about me. I'm supposed to keep my little brothers in line and show them a good example.

ESHA: You get loads of freedom.

FAROOQ: Hanging at Juicys, skiving school don't bother him, as long as Tariq, Rafiq and Shafiq don't try it. But if I was to bring any disrespect on the family, I'd be on the first plane to Pakistan.

ESHA: No!

FAROOQ: I'm not going to get in line for that ticket man. Your dad's too strict with you though, he'd chop your balls off.

ESHA: He's out of order. It's like he's keeping me in line 'cause he stepped out of line.

FAROOQ: What did he do?

ESHA shrugs his shoulders.

ESHA: Got married young, but like it was love and they went against the family. They've never been back to India, or even written to them.

FAROOQ: Weird.

ESHA: Maybe. I'm not really bothered. I'm sick of their arguing about who wanted to come here and who didn't, and my mum crying and him ignoring her. Farooq, did you ever dream about your dad?

FAROOQ: Don't be soft, I don't dream.

ESHA is taken aback.

ESHA: Never?

FAROOQ: Well I don't remember any. Do you?

ESHA: Nah.

FAROOQ: What you asking for then?

ESHA: Dunno. **(Pause)** I had this dream last night that I was eating my dad.

FAROOQ: Eating him? Weird man. Tell me.

ESHA: Nah.

FAROOQ: Go on. Eat him.

ESHA: It was like I was at this lakeside and I was walking in the dark, I couldn't find my way, everything was blurry. Suddenly this buffalo came out of the water, looking all around. I knew it was my dad. I ran forward and swung this large sword and cut off his head. Then I made a fire and roasted and ate him. There was blood everywhere and I was really full, but I kept eating.

FAROOQ: Gross!

ESHA: Do you think it's stupid?

FAROOQ: Dunno.

ESHA: What do you think it means?

FAROOQ: Dreams don't mean nothing, it's just watching a film before you go to bed and it giving you dreams, that's all.

ESHA: What film have you seen that shit in?

FAROOQ shrugs his shoulders.

ESHA: I just don't want to end up like him.

FAROOQ: He's all right sometimes.

ESHA: He's me dad, he winds me up.

FAROOQ: I definitely don't want to end up like my old man.

ESHA: Well we won't if we don't want to. Shake on it.

FAROOQ and ESHA shake hands and then slap them.

ESHA: Why don't boys talk to each other?

FAROOQ: You never shut up! (**Laughs**) What you saying?

ESHA: It's not the same how boys are, compared to girls, how they are together.

FAROOQ: Who wants to be like those gossiping giggling girls!

ESHA: I thought you liked girls?

FAROOQ: Yeah, one girl, not them all! What's the big deal?

ESHA gestures with his hands.

ESHA: Imagine a football game, we're here, the girls are here in opposition — *(and you've got possession of the ball)*.

FAROOQ: An' you try to tackle one, you go in too hard and you end up with the whole of the opposition giving you a licking. Is that what you're saying?

ESHA: Never mind, you don't understand footie, it's more strategic than that.

FAROOQ: And you don't understand girls, there's strategies for them too.

ESHA: What strategies?

FAROOQ: Get one and you'll find out.

FAROOQ smirks at ESHA.

FAROOQ: I'm off to Juicys. (**Pause**) Hey, come with me, I've arranged to meet Kaahini.

ESHA: Nah, I gotta train.

FAROOQ: I told her about you. Come on, I want you to meet her.

ESHA: Yeah man, you want me to cramp your style.

FAROOQ: Later.

FAROOQ strides off. ESHA throws himself on the ground and does five squat thrusts.

ESHA: Tell Pinkie if he touches you he's dead.

FAROOQ: No worries. I can look after myself man.

ESHA rolls over, does five press-ups, rolls over and does five sit-ups, and struggles to his feet. FAROOQ watches ESHA from the shadows of the alleyway.
   NEELENDRA sneaks up behind ESHA, he grabs him round the throat with his arm. ESHA grabs the arm and pulls his dad over his shoulder and slams him on the ground. FAROOQ smiles and then saunters off.

NEELENDRA: Oof.

ESHA: Dad! I could've mashed you up.

NEELENDRA: Sorry son, I was just testing your reflexes.

NEELENDRA gets up and brushes down his clothes.

ESHA: Have I passed the test then?

NEELENDRA: Flying colours. How's the training going?

ESHA: I'm captain.

NEELENDRA: Great.

ESHA: We've still got some tactics to practise before the game. But it's coming together nicely.

NEELENDRA: We're gonna win then?

ESHA: Definitely.

ESHA toes the football into the air and headers it towards his dad. NEELENDRA headers it back to him.

ESHA: Not bad, for a beginner.

NEELENDRA gestures for ESHA to header the football back. ESHA does.

ESHA: You on nights?

NEELENDRA: Plenty of time to get to work. Come on.

NEELENDRA headers the ball to the ground and dribbles it towards ESHA. ESHA tackles him and wins the ball easily. ESHA dribbles towards the wall and boots the ball hard.

ESHA: Goal! One nil.

NEELENDRA retrieves the ball and dribbles towards ESHA, ESHA tackles him, NEELENDRA pushes him out of the way, ESHA falls to the ground. NEELENDRA retrieves the ball and kicks it hard at the wall.

NEELENDRA: Goal, one all.

The football ricochets off the wall and hits ESHA in the chest, he writhes on the ground in agony.

ESHA: (**gasps**) Shit man! That was a foul!

NEELENDRA: You okay son?

ESHA staggers to his feet.

NEELENDRA: You big girl!

NEELENDRA puts his arm awkwardly around ESHA's shoulders. ESHA pulls away and brushes himself off.

ESHA: No broken bones.

NEELENDRA: After the final you need to get down to some serious studying.

ESHA: You're always deciding that shit. I am studying hard.

NEELENDRA: You don't get anywhere these days without a string of A's.

ESHA: But I don't want to go anywhere that needs A's.

NEELENDRA: You can't play football all your life.

ESHA: I don't even know if I want to do a finance degree.

NEELENDRA: Don't argue with me. Your future's important, to us all. Your mum and I lost our chance for education so don't mess it up.

ESHA: How can I decide about my whole life now?

NEELENDRA: Decisions have to be made. That's the way of life.

ESHA: All right, all right, I'll get a form from careers tomorrow. What about you dad, did you know what you wanted to be at sixteen?

NEELENDRA: I thought I did, but that was a long time ago. You don't want to make my mistakes over again.

ESHA: What mistakes?

NEELENDRA picks up the football and throws it hard at ESHA. ESHA catches it.

NEELENDRA: Better make tracks.

ESHA: Dad.

NEELENDRA: Yes.

ESHA: Do you love mum?

NEELENDRA: Of course I do! Don't be silly. If it's because of the arguing your mum and I have argued our whole marriage. She's stubborn, that's all, leave your mum to me and you concentrate on winning the match, okay.

ESHA sprints off.

ESHA: Okay, the match.

Scene 11

ANISHAA sits at the kitchen table, she wears an apron over her salwaar kameez. She reads *The Sun* newspaper whilst massaging her feet; she tries to avoid Page 3.

ESHA, dressed in the red salwaar kameez and duputta, tries to rush past ANISHAA. ANISHAA jumps up when she sees ESHA and grabs his arm.

ANISHAA: Esha! What the hell do you think you're playing at?

ESHA looks down, but is grinning.

ESHA: Nothing.

ANISHAA: Get my salwaar kameez off, and while you're at it you can take that look off your face.

ESHA: I needed it to . . . (*I can't explain*).

ANISHAA: And I needed you to tell your dad.

ESHA: Me tell him, what about you?

ANISHAA: If you'd backed me up.

ESHA: You didn't want to know about it a few days ago.

ANISHAA: You have no idea, no idea what it's been like, what I have been through for you.

ESHA: For me? Don't tell me this whole . . . (*charade*) was for me. More like you did it for yourself.

ANISHAA holds her belly as if she's remembering Esha's birth, then she grips it like she's tearing her womb out.

ANISHAA: We've both lied now, so you've no choice but to get on with being a son.

ESHA: Choice! What choice?

ANISHAA: You should have told him.

ESHA: I just didn't tell him my, that *it* had started, that's all.

ANISHAA: You still lied.

ESHA: I can't ignore how I feel mum.

ANISHAA: I've been doing it for years. Neelendra has a son and he'd have a fit if he saw you dressed up like . . .

ANISHAA grabs the duputta from around ESHA's shoulders. ESHA glares at ANISHAA. ANISHAA pushes ESHA towards the mirror.

ANISHAA: . . . a Hijra.

ESHA turns away from the mirror.

ESHA: You made me this way, why didn't you do something about it before now?

ANISHAA: I've told you, I was young, confused about what was important and, that dream about . . . (*the buffalo*).

ESHA: A fucken dream! Get real mum.

ANISHAA: Your dad mistook you for a son and . . . (*then I couldn't tell him*).

ESHA: I'll never understand how it happened.

ANISHAA takes the end of the red duputta and tries to rub the lipstick from ESHA's mouth.

ANISHAA: Wearing my kameez does not make you my daughter.

ESHA: But I am your . . . (*daughter*).

ANISHAA: It's too late now. You don't understand about your dad, being lied to is the one thing he never forgives.

ESHA: Can't you talk to him?

ANISHAA: You had your chance. I don't want to see you dressed like this again, if you do your father'll know about it.

ESHA: You can't.

ANISHAA: Try me.

ESHA: Mum.

ANISHAA: Mum nothing, if you want to be his son so badly then you can get on with it.

ESHA: I don't know what I want.

ANISHAA: You've had chances we never had. Think about your cup final.

ESHA: Winning, what good is that now I can't be who — (*I am*).

NEELENDRA walks along the alleyway. ANISHAA hears his footsteps.

ANISHAA: Your dad's back. There's no turning back now, quick go upstairs.

ESHA: Go on, push me away like you do dad.

ESHA goes towards the back door.

ESHA: I'm out of here.

ANISHAA pushes ESHA away.

ANISHAA: Esha get upstairs before he sees you.

NEELENDRA enters the kitchen.

ANISHAA: What you doing home?

NEELENDRA: I forgot my glasses. I see you found your red kameez. Changed your mind then?

ANISHAA: What?

ANISHAA looks at the red duputta, she crumples it up and stuffs it into the pocket of her apron.

NEELENDRA: Where was it?

ANISHAA: What?

NEELENDRA: Never mind. Is Esha home?

ANISHAA: I think he's upstairs, changing.

NEELENDRA: I thought mothers always knew where their sons were?

ANISHAA: Sometimes.

NEELENDRA: Nisha, what you up to?

ANISHAA: What you talking about?

NEELENDRA: Anishaa, is there something I should know?

ANISHAA: What do you mean?

NEELENDRA: Has Esha told you something he can't tell me?

ANISHAA: You know what boys are like at this age, they can't talk about their feelings.

NEELENDRA: He's close to Farooq, isn't he?

ANISHAA: Yes of course.

NEELENDRA: How close?

ANISHAA: I don't know, they do everything together, have done since they could walk.

NEELENDRA: Everything?

ANISHAA: Neelendra, what are you getting at? Spit it out.

NEELENDRA: Is he, is he a (**pause**) homosexual.

ANISHAA: (**laughs**) Homosexual! Of course not, where did you get that idea from?

NEELENDRA: Thank god, thank god, you know, he's never talked about girls, I thought he wasn't, normal.

ANISHAA: Too busy running around after a ball.

NEELENDRA: Yes, that's it, he's too busy for girls.

NEELENDRA picks up his glasses and walks off. ANISHAA watches him go.

Scene 12

FAROOQ saunters across the alleyway, he looks at his reflection in the side of an old railway carriage, combs his hair and adjusts his clothes.

KAAHINI/ESHA, in her red salwaar kameez and duputta, turns the corner, sees **FAROOQ** and starts to walk in the opposite direction.

FAROOQ: (**shouts**) Kaahini, wait.

KAAHINI/ESHA stops and turns towards FAROOQ as he catches her up.

FAROOQ: Kaahini! Where were you last night?

KAAHINI/ESHA: I couldn't get out, my mum kept me in.

FAROOQ: Why?

KAAHINI/ESHA: I don't know, she just did.

FAROOQ: Where are you going?

KAAHINI/ESHA: Why d'you have to ask so many questions?

FAROOQ: Sorry. Is there something wrong?

KAAHINI/ESHA: I don't know, no, yes, everything's wrong. Look, I'm not sure if I can see you again Farooq, I can't keep sneaking out, someone's gonna find out. If anyone found us together we'd be dead.

FAROOQ: You mean 'cause we're (**pause**) different?

KAAHINI/ESHA: Something like that sh . . . (*it*)

FAROOQ: You're a Hindu aren't you?

KAAHINI/ESHA: Yes, and you're a Muslim.

FAROOQ: That's nothing, I won't let that stand between me and you. I'm not bothered what my family think.

KAAHINI/ESHA: Yeah, maybe, but they'll blackmail you into doing what they want anyway.

FAROOQ: Is she really strict your mum?

KAAHINI/ESHA: She just wants me (**pause**) married, that's as far as it goes. I've got to go.

FAROOQ: Have they found someone?

KAAHINI/ESHA: It's none of your business.

FAROOQ: Is that why you want to finish it?

KAAHINI/ESHA: Stop interrogating me. I don't want to talk about it.

FAROOQ: Let's talk about us. Do you think I could be right for you?

FAROOQ approaches KAAHINI/ESHA.

KAAHINI/ESHA: Things are more complicated than that. It's not just — (*about you*)

FAROOQ: What?

KAAHINI/ESHA: I can't get involved.

FAROOQ: But I love you.

KAAHINI/ESHA: Love me? How can you?

FAROOQ: I just do, you've got to see me again. We'll meet at midnight or something.

KAAHINI/ESHA: I'm scared.

FAROOQ: I'll look after you.

KAAHINI/ESHA: Farooq.

FAROOQ: Yeah.

KAAHINI/ESHA: I want to ask you something.

FAROOQ: What?

KAAHINI/ESHA: If you had to choose between your family and love, what would you choose?

FAROOQ: I told you, love.

KAAHINI/ESHA: Between something you loved and love?

FAROOQ: Love again.

KAAHINI/ESHA: Between friendship and love?

FAROOQ: I don't know. Why?

KAAHINI/ESHA: Just wondering.

ANISHAA runs down the alleyway. KAAHINI/ESHA spots her and sprints off in the other direction.

FAROOQ: Kaahini, wait!

FAROOQ tries to run after KAAHINI/ESHA. ANISHAA grabs FAROOQ.

ANISHAA: Farooq, have you seen Esha?

FAROOQ: No. He said he was training.

ANISHAA: I need to talk to him. Who was that you were with?

FAROOQ: Oh, no one, just a girl from school.

ANISHAA: In a salwaar?

FAROOQ: Please don't tell my mum, Mrs Annand. We're just friends. It's just, you know, my parents would get the wrong idea.

ANISHAA: Well I'm not sure if I approve, was that a red salwaar kameez she was wearing?

FAROOQ: Yes. Why?

ANISHAA: Farooq, I want you to swear that you'll never see this girl again.

FAROOQ: No!

ANISHAA: You must, it's important to me.

FAROOQ: To you? I can't not see her again Mrs Annand. I love her.

ANISHAA: What do you know of love at your age?

FAROOQ: But you fell in l . . . (*ove*)

ANISHAA looks at FAROOQ suspiciously.

ANISHAA: If you don't stop seeing her, I'll tell your father.

FAROOQ: But he'll kill me, you can't do this to me.

ANISHAA: I don't have a choice, I have to do my duty.

FAROOQ: Your husband thinks it's okay to have girlfriends, I'm going to tell him, he can say — (*if its all right*)

FAROOQ turns to go.

ANISHAA: No! Don't do that Farooq, he's busy at work and anyway he has troubles of his own with (**pause**) Esha.

FAROOQ: Esha?

ANISHAA: You mustn't bother Esha's dad, he'd agree with me that you shouldn't be seeing this girl.

FAROOQ walks briskly away.

FAROOQ: I'll let him decide.

ANISHAA follows and tries to grab **FAROOQ**, he turns to face her defiantly, she withdraws her hand.

ANISHAA: Farooq.

FAROOQ leaps across the railway level-crossing. **ANISHAA** collapses in a heap on the train track and looks in both directions.

Scene 13

FAROOQ runs down the alley. **KAAHINI/ESHA** runs across the alleyway looking behind her. They run into each other.

FAROOQ: Thank god I've found you. Why did you run off?

KAAHINI/ESHA: I thought someone'd caught us.

FAROOQ: She did. Esha's mum, she was going bananas. She's gonna tell my dad unless I stop seeing you.

KAAHINI/ESHA: You can't risk that.

FAROOQ: I can't risk losing you.

KAAHINI/ESHA: What did she see?

FAROOQ: I dunno, she was going on about it being important to her, doing her duty.

KAAHINI/ESHA: Your dad'd go spare.

FAROOQ: I told you, I don't care. Anyway I've had a better idea.

KAAHINI/ESHA: I've got to go, maybe she'll come back.

FAROOQ: Listen. We'll go to Esha's dad Mr Annand, he'll know what to do, I can trust him.

KAAHINI/ESHA: No we can't.

FAROOQ: Why? What you scared of?

KAAHINI/ESHA: He'll tell and then you'll be packed off to Pakistan.

FAROOQ: How did you know that?

KAAHINI/ESHA: What?

FAROOQ: That they'd pack me off?

KAAHINI/ESHA: It's obvious. Look, we can't trust anyone.

FAROOQ: Do you trust me?

KAAHINI/ESHA: I suppose.

FAROOQ: Well then, believe me, I know him, it's the right thing to do.

KAAHINI/ESHA: I can't.

FAROOQ: You have to, it's our only chance. Prove to me that you — (*love me*)

KAAHINI/ESHA: I can't see you any more, I told you, it's getting too risky, this was bound to happen.

FAROOQ: Don't give up on us. I swear to you this is the most important thing that's ever happened to me. Is it because you don't love me?

FAROOQ takes KAAHINI/ESHA's hand and kisses it.

KAAHINI/ESHA: Farooq, turn around.

FAROOQ: No, you'll run away.

KAAHINI/ESHA: I won't, I promise. Just for a minute, and shut your eyes.

FAROOQ turns away from KAAHINI/ESHA. She takes off the red salwaar kameez and duputta and is revealed as ESHA in her tracksuit.

ESHA: You can turn back.

FAROOQ turns and sees ESHA, he stares fiercely at him. ESHA shuts his eyes.

FAROOQ: You sick bastard!

FAROOQ spits and rubs his mouth viciously with the back of his hand.

ESHA: Stop it!

ESHA takes a step closer to FAROOQ.

FAROOQ: Get away from me you pervert.

FAROOQ spits again.

FAROOQ: What are you doing?

ESHA: You must have known it was me.

FAROOQ: It wasn't you, it was, it was . . . What the fucks going on?

ESHA: I can explain.

FAROOQ: Don't bother, it's obvious.

FAROOQ spins around and runs off down the alleyway, ESHA watches him go, then walks off into the distance.

Scene 14

NEELENDRA stands at one end of the railway track with his torch and work bag in his hands. ANISHAA runs towards him.

NEELENDRA: What are you doing here?

ANISHAA: (**breathless**) I have to talk to you.

NEELENDRA: But here? I'm due to take a train out.

ANISHAA: It can't wait.

NEELENDRA: Is Esha all right?

ANISHAA: No, I mean yes. I mean I think he's okay but we need to talk about him, us.

NEELENDRA: What's happened? Tell me.

ANISHAA: Nothing, everything. Neelendra listen to me. Remember when we were just married and you had that dream — (*about the buffalo*)

NEELENDRA: Nisha, if it's just all that stuff again you can tell me later. If I'm late it'll put the timetables out and then I'll be in serious trouble.

ANISHAA: We went to the fair. It was a beautiful evening and we held hands, were full of expectation and longing, desire scarlet as the setting sun. We were so young.

NEELENDRA stands awkwardly, looking around to see if anyone's listening.

NEELENDRA: That was so long ago, tell me another time, I'll listen I promise.

ANISHAA: Then I spotted that Mystic doing fortunes and we needed to know that we'd done the right thing. I whispered,

'Let's see what life has in store for us.' There was a bright orange flame and the shadow of you being sceptical, in the end you told him your dream. You said you'd prayed for an end to your worries, and the Mystic said the dream was an answer to your prayers. And somehow you thought he meant you'd have a son, and you thought that was the answer. And it turned out he was right about one thing, I was pregnant. But your family were even more hostile to me, like I'd got pregnant to take you away from them. I thought it didn't matter. But then there was all that blood, I was screaming out for you, I couldn't find you in the darkness.

ANISHAA looks up, NEELENDRA is staring at her transfixed, ANISHAA pleads with her eyes for forgiveness.

ANISHAA: And the next day suddenly there you were in the doorway, hazy and then becoming clearer. You came in and said, 'Give me my son.' I gazed down at her, looked deep into her brown eyes, and then stared across at your eyes, vast pools swimming with love for me, and I looked up and said (**pause**) — (*take him*).

ANISHAA is trembling. NEELENDRA holds open his arms to take an imaginary baby from ANISHAA, she places the baby in his arms.

NEELENDRA: And you said, 'Take him'. And I took him from your arms and held him tight.

NEELENDRA looks down.

NEELENDRA: No.

NEELENDRA thrusts the baby back into ANISHAA's arms, she holds the baby tightly and shields her from NEELENDRA.

ANISHAA: You didn't want to know.

NEELENDRA: You lied to me.

ANISHAA: Yourself.

NEELENDRA: Why didn't you say?

ANISHAA: What could I say? Your dream.

NEELENDRA: It was just a dream.

ANISHAA: Didn't know how to, what to say. I said what I thought you wanted to hear. I just had my womb ripped out from me, for god's sake. I was never going to have that son you wanted.

ANISHAA turns back towards NEELENDRA, she holds out the baby in her arms, NEELENDRA dashes the baby to the ground. ANISHAA drops to her knees with her arms outstretched towards him.

ANISHAA: You killed her!

NEELENDRA: Him, there never was a her.

ANISHAA runs off. NEELENDRA stares along the railway track into the distance.

FAROOQ walks along the railway tracks, hands outstretched like he's trying to balance, he spies NEELENDRA and shouts to him across the tracks.

FAROOQ: (**shouts**) Oi Mr Annand, I need to talk to you.

NEELENDRA: Not now Farooq.

FAROOQ: Your son's got a problem with women's clothes, or don't you know.

NEELENDRA: What are you talking about? Women's clothes?

FAROOQ: It's obvious, the wanker.

NEELENDRA: My god, what's been going on?

FAROOQ: You are all perverted, bastards!

NEELENDRA: Farooq please. I didn't know.

FAROOQ stares vehemently at NEELENDRA, NEELENDRA wants to walk away, but can't.

FAROOQ: I'll never forgive him for this.

NEELENDRA: . . . Farooq.

FAROOQ: What you going on about?

NEELENDRA: I just thought that Anishaa needed time to heal.

FAROOQ: I should have known, all that dreaming and shit.

NEELENDRA: I thought she was homesick, 'Remember the dream', she'd say.

FAROOQ: (**rants**) Dream, fuck . . .

NEELENDRA: I thought the weather made her depressed.

FAROOQ: . . . fuckin' weather . . .

NEELENDRA: I never realised it was her illness. We just ignored each other and got further and further apart until we were barely together, just living our lives in parallel. I didn't understand where the love went.

FAROOQ: What you telling me?

NEELENDRA: I wanted my parents to be proud of me. Was I wrong to want something so badly that I couldn't see the truth.

FAROOQ: The truth is your son's fuckin' bent.

NEELENDRA: Not my son.

FAROOQ: He likes dressing up in girls' clothes, so what is he then? Your fuckin' daughter?

NEELENDRA looks away.

FAROOQ: No! I would have known! He's been my friend since, forever. It was because he, didn't want a girlfriend or something. Didn't want to choose with his training, didn't want to lose the cup.

NEELENDRA: Why couldn't I see?

FAROOQ: Since forever, climbing trees. He's even seen my . . . (*dick*)

NEELENDRA: Farooq, I just wanted you to know the truth.

FAROOQ: What fuckin' truth? It's all lies.

NEELENDRA: I'm sorry.

FAROOQ: He hurt me, not she, he, I hate him.

FAROOQ starts to walk away.

NEELENDRA: The first time, I can't explain. After that we were deceiving each other without even knowing it.

NEELENDRA watches FAROOQ run into the distance, he turns and faces the opposite direction.

ESHA, holding her Nike bag, walks along the railway track trying to balance. NEELENDRA watches her approach. ESHA stops and looks at him, NEELENDRA continues walking.

Scene 15

NEELENDRA, dressed in his train-drivers uniform, walks into the kitchen. ANISHAA kneads dough at the table.

ANISHAA: Do you want roti?

NEELENDRA: Not hungry.

ANISHAA: I can make if you want.

ANISHAA kneads the dough and starts to make rotia regardless.

NEELENDRA: Not hungry, didn't you hear me?

ANISHAA: Shall I wait for Esha then?

NEELENDRA: There is no Esha.

ANISHAA sits down at the table and sobs into her hands smearing flour over her face. NEELENDRA ignores her and stares at the uncooked rotia.

NEELENDRA: Didn't you hear what I said?

ANISHAA runs out of the kitchen. NEELENDRA turns to face the Krishna shrine.

Scene 16

KAAHINI, dressed in the red duputta, kicks her football against the wall in the alley. The ball ricochets and she slams it hard into the wall, it comes back and almost knocks her off her feet.

KAAHINI: I don't want some hand-me-down second-hand costume.

KAAHINI empties her Nike bag onto the railway track. There's the red salwaar kameez, her school football strip, an old toy train, an exercise book, an old Indian doll wearing a sari and an old photograph of an Asian girl. KAAHINI rummages through her things, examining each item.

KAAHINI: I don't know what I want, I can't decide.

KAAHINI rips pages from the exercise book, lights them, watches them catch fire and start to burn.
    NEELENDRA walks tentatively towards the Krishna shrine, head bowed, holy book in his hands. NEELENDRA lights a candle on the shrine and faces it, opens the book and recites from the Gita.

NEELENDRA: Know with Soul
    Unborn, undying,
    Never ceasing,
    Never beginning,

KAAHINI: When I was young
    I wanted to
    be strong,
    drive a train
    like my dad,

NEELENDRA: Deathless, birthless,
    Unchanging for ever

KAAHINI: be my own man,

NEELENDRA: How can it die
    The death of the body?

KAAHINI: hurtling into
   the black night.

KAAHINI throws her school football strip into the flames.

NEELENDRA: Knowing it birthless,

KAAHINI: How do I remember
   my childhood
   now?

NEELENDRA: Knowing it deathless,
   Knowing it endless,

KAAHINI: Do I have to
   rewrite it,

NEELENDRA: Forever unchanging,

KAAHINI: edit out
   the train-set,

NEELENDRA: Dream not you do
   The deed of the killer,
   Dream not the power
   Is yours to command it.

KAAHINI: the football team?

KAAHINI throws the kameez into the flames.

NEELENDRA: Worn-out garments
   Are shed by the body,

KAAHINI: Who
   am
   I
   now?

NEELENDRA: Worn-out bodies
   Are shed by the dweller

KAAHINI: Am I
    a girl

NEELENDRA: Within the body,

KAAHINI: in a boy's
    personality?

NEELENDRA: New bodies are donned
    By the dweller,
    Like garments.

KAAHINI throws an Indian doll wearing a sari into the flames, then retrieves it before it burns.

NEELENDRA: Not dried, not wetted,
    Not burned, not wounded,

KAAHINI: Beneath my skin
    a woman has been
    growing

NEELENDRA: Innermost element,
    Everywhere, always,
    Being of beings,
    Changeless, eternal

KAAHINI: What is this male
    power

NEELENDRA: For ever and ever.

Neelendra sits frozen with grief.

KAAHINI: that slips so easily
    with my mask
    and becomes ashes?
    Freedom is nothing left to lose.

The ashes scatter. KAAHINI picks up her toy train, the doll

and the photograph, puts them in her Nike bag.

KAAHINI strides across the alleyway, retrieves her football, and stands in the middle of the level crossing. She ties the duputta around her head like a bandanna.

KAAHINI: The 4.19 where could you take me, Leeds, Bradford, that won't be far enough, 'cause I don't exist here any more.

FAROOQ watches from the shadows of the alleyway, he cautiously approaches KAAHINI.

FAROOQ: You're a girl and you fought Pinkie for me. I can't get it right in my head.

KAAHINI: Yeah well, I'm stronger than you.

FAROOQ: (**whispers**) Your dad told me.

KAAHINI: What does it matter now. You hate me.

FAROOQ: You lied.

KAAHINI: Lied to yourself. What about my bag?

FAROOQ looks away.

FAROOQ: I dunno what I thought. What will you do?

KAAHINI: Now I've burnt . . . dunno, I can hardly appear on the field on Sunday with a half-burnt strip on.

FAROOQ: Borrow one, no one'd know about . . . (*that you're a girl*).

KAAHINI: I know.

FAROOQ: But the cup?

KAAHINI: I know I could play, and we'd win, but I'm not playing by the rules, so what's the point of scoring now? Take this.

KAAHINI hands FAROOQ her football, FAROOQ tries to give it back.

KAAHINI: Just keep it safe for me. Will you visit them?

FAROOQ: If you want me to.

KAAHINI nods yes.

FAROOQ: Your dad, he's all right.

KAAHINI: He likes you.

FAROOQ: I trusted you.

KAAHINI: Am I really so different today from who I was two weeks ago?

FAROOQ: That wasn't a proper girl, it was you dressed up.

KAAHINI: That's who I am, if you loved her then you loved me.

FAROOQ: Who are you, Kaahini or Esha?

ESHA: It's not the name that matters, I don't know anymore. I just want to be whoever's been trapped under this lie for sixteen years.

FAROOQ: I don't know who you are, but I still . . . *(love you)*

ESHA: You're the best friend I ever had.

FAROOQ: If . . . *(you want to stay)*

ESHA: I don't even know what's possible, except leaving and trying to find . . . *(whatever's missing)*

ESHA turns to go.

FAROOQ: Esha . . . I'll miss you.

Kaahini

ESHA playfully does a mock punch towards FAROOQ's belly. FAROOQ grabs her hand, they look at each other. FAROOQ almost kisses ESHA, she pulls away.

ESHA: You don't even know me.

End

The Life of Stuff
Simon Donald

Sex, drugs and Frank Sinatra: The Life of Stuff is a brilliantly funny fly-on-the-wall snapshot of eight lives careering out of control as small-time crook and aspirant pharmaceutical entrepreneur Willie Dobie's best laid plans unravel when human nature takes its predictably unpredictable course... In common with a number of first-rate modern Scottish plays The Life of Stuff has, as yet, only received two professional productions. I fervently hope this new publication will lead to the wider recognition it deserves.

Hugh Hodgart, Head of Acting at RSAMD, Glasgow

Furiously contemporary, extremely funny and has a cast of outrageous yet sympathetic characters which take possession like a cult.

Julie Morrice, Scotland on Sunday

ISBN 0-9545206-6-1

£5.99

Available from Booksource Tel: 0870 240 2182
and www.capercailliebooks.co.uk

The Waltzer

Rhiannon Tise

The Waltzer is a touching and sensitive exploration of the serious business of growing up. A world of beleaguered single parents and adolescent fears and friendships is reflected in the dark mirror of Sally's experience on her first real date. The garish glamour and hectic motion of the fairground and the Waltzer itself provide a perfect setting for this multi-faceted depiction of the thrills and spills of a teenager's first steps towards the adult world. Written for radio, The Waltzer draws much of its power and point from the complex interaction between past and present events, inner monologue and intercut dialogue. In our film and TV dominated culture we can easily miss out on the imaginative strength of radio drama – the publication of this play is a timely reminder of the real alternatives to the siren call of MTV, Cartoon Network and the Disney Channel.

Hugh Hodgart, Head of Acting at RSAMD, Glasgow

ISBN 0-9545206-3-7

£5.99

Available from Booksource Tel: 0870 240 2182 and www.capercailliebooks.co.uk

King Matt

Stephen Greenhorn

King Matt, the story of a boy who becomes a king, is a simple fable filled with surprisingly complex resonances. In common with the very best in storytelling for children, it confronts the big moral issues surrounding the way in which one makes one's way in the world and through life: self-interest vying with self-sacrifice, the greed of the individual with the needs of the collective. The boy-king Matt is undoubtedly the hero of the tale but it is his human faults and frailties as well as his intrepid spirit that keep us on the edge of our seats right up to the suspense-filled ending. This is a play written for children that children would have great fun playing for themselves.

Hugh Hodgart, Head of Acting at RSAMD, Glasgow

A highly articulate play that speaks volumes about the nature of democracy and personal responisibility.

The Stage

ISBN 0-9545206-2-9

£5.99

Available from Booksource Tel: 0870 240 2182
and www.capercailliebooks.co.uk

Dr Korczak's Example

David Greig

Dr Korczak's Example is set in the final, numbered, days of an orphanage in the Warsaw ghetto in 1942. Based on real events, this 'Brechtian' retelling generates an almost unbearable power and pathos through the simple humanity, warts and all, of the central characters who are trapped both by the inexorable forces of Nazi oppression and by our fore-knowledge of the fate that awaits them. The play's 'alienation' device of depicting its characters through the use of dolls, further enhances our painful feeling of powerlessness. Yet, in spite of its tragic outcome, Dr Korczak's Example, like the real life of its protagonist, leaves us exhilarated and uplifted by the indomitable power of love.

Hugh Hodgart, Head of Acting at RSAMD, Glasgow

This is the dramatist's art turned to serve an idea of theatre which is unreproducable in any other medium – a play not to forget.

Will Hutton, The Observer

ISBN 0-9545206-1-0

£5.99

Available from Booksource Tel: 0870 240 2182
and www.capercailliebooks.co.uk

Sunburst Finish

Andrea Gibb
Paddy Cunneen

'Note to self. You are dying.' As a young man's depression turns to despair, suicide seems the only way out - the only way to take control. In spite of the bleakness of its subject, *Sunburst Finish* is filled with strong and vibrant voices, a rich mosaic of music, wit, warmth, insight, feeling, and a remarkable lack of sentimentality. The central character's struggle to come to terms with himself and the world around him is one that all young (and not so young) people will relate strongly to.

Hugh Hodgart, Head of Acting at RSAMD, Glasgow

ISBN 0-9545206-5-3

£5.99

Available from Booksource Tel: 0870 240 2182 and www.capercailliebooks.co.uk

Shakespeare The Director's Cut

Michael Bogdanov

This collection of cutting-edge essays is a valuable addition to Shakespeare studies, and to theatre studies more generally. Michael Bogdanov's cuts are always incisive, razor-sharp, and applied with an unerring hand. Never dogmatic or programmatic, Bogdanov approaches each play attentive to its novelty and its nuances, alive to its urgency and impact, attuned to its language and its lore. As a director acutely aware of critical conventions – enough to want to overturn them – Bogdanov is uniquely positioned to combine theoretical acuity with a practitioner's knowledge of what works on the page and in performance, while never losing sight of what is most politically resonant and socially engaged. The meat is moist closest to the bone, and these are choice cuts from a master butcher.

Willy Maley, Professor of Renaissance Studies,
University of Glasgow

For 30 years Michael Bogdanov has been the most consistently interesting and provocative of British directors of Shakespeare. Now he has written a series of incisive essays on the plays – not comments on his many productions, but introductions to the works that show the result of his long acquaintance with them. The essays, based in social thought and theatrical savvy, make Shakespeare accessible and immediate and will be of interest to a wide range of readers.

Dennis Kennedy, Beckett Professor of Drama,
Trinity College Dublin

Michael Bogdanov is the Tyrone Guthrie of our day, and his signature is all over the work of many young directors. He is at once scholar, provocateur, puritan and Lord of Misrule.

Michael Pennington

ISBN 0-9545206-0-2

£8.99

Available from Booksource Tel: 0870 240 2182
and www.capercailliebooks.co.uk
From all major bookshops and www.amazon.co.uk